Wandering Eyes
and Other Poems

Aileen Gallagher

Golden Antelope Press
Kirksville, Missouri
2009

©2009 by Aileen Gallagher

All rights reserved. No portion of this publication may be duplicated in any way without the expressed written consent of the publisher, except in the form of brief excerpts or quotations for review purposes.

ISBN: 978-0-9817902-1-3 (0-9817902-1-6)

Library of Congress Control Number: 2009935254

Published by:

Golden Antelope Press
715 E. McPherson St.
Kirksville, Missouri 63501
Phone: (660) 665-0273
manager@golden-antelope-press.com

Wandering Eyes
and
Other Poems

Contents

An Invocation	7
Wandering Eyes	11
Goodbye	13
Forgive Me	15
Observations of a Generous Man	20
Idel Hands	21
As I Sit Here	23
Lonely Again	24
An Object of My Affection	25
Communion	26
Reflection	30
Such is My Love	32
Deprivation	34
At an Interface	37
Confessions in the Dark	39
Worn Braille	41
It Is This Way	43
A Seed	45
A Lullaby *for Sean*	46
A Lullaby (Lesson 2) *for Sean*	47
Perennial Forces	48
Potential Energy	49
A Christening	51
A Transient Anger	53
Catch 22	55
Death By A Thousand Cuts	57
A Diminished Thing	61

An Invocation

Pious lips move tirelessly,
Pronouncing prayers
Whose winding wants and pleas
And honorable poetry spiral
Toward heaven. Millions move their
Thoughts in this direction, begging for

Mercy in genuflecting introspection.
Many, too, are thankful
Polishing their prayers
Like gems, raw and ripe
With hurt and with shame and with pride.
Millions now are doing this.

Imagine then God's great ears,
Her infamous omniscient mind
Turning in all directions,
Receiving each silent thought with
Great equanimity.
Imagine, too, your dying thoughts

Being caught in Her great web of
Greater thought.
Imagine this, then, that we
Are never alone in our suffering,

That despite our distance from
Each other, the spaces we have

Opened and placed there,
Despite our isolating pain and
Perpetual petty sins, that God
Walks, breaths, listens
At our sides, close enough to hear
All we mumble under our breaths,

So close we need never to sing
Her praises, but only think them,
Only thank Her and ask forgiveness
For our limits.
Again, listen: gentle lips fumble
Over the correct words… The

Greatest wound of all severs mouths
Open into pairs whose noxious
Noise clamors in inadequate
Clouds of prayer.
I stand silently aside,
Whisper nothing of

My despair, for
I have nothing to say.
(What's said that hasn't already
Been sung? Peace lives on a
Quiet tongue.)
This is how I pray…

To no one in particular,

Not even to myself,
Brooding behind
Wandering eyes…
I mutter reassurances with furious,
Febrile haste.

Weary and anxious and alone,
I write from inside claustrophobic
Walls and think from inside
The tightening tediums of thoughts,
The hard, cool skull full of transgressions,
Indecisions; practiced inhibitions

No longer remain reliable when
I'm in these states.
I—an interesting specimen,
Redundant though unpredictable,
My thoughts reverberating
On these pages.

I invite you in, reluctantly,
For I am in need of company.

Wandering Eyes

And the man . . . poor . . . poor!
He turns his eyes around, like
when patting calls us upon our shoulder;
he turns his crazed maddened eyes,
and all of life's experiences become stagnant, like a puddle of
    guilt, in a daze.

--- *The Black Messengers* Cesar Vallejo

With a sly, sideways
                         glancing stare
I saw the scene
                    unfold—not told
directly, but with daring,
                      glaring speculation
I saw it all…
                    despite my cautious,
feigned fascination
            with the boring blackness
burning in my cup.
                      I saw him first,
the flailing arms,
                  the stern stubble,
the clumsy voice,
            all catching my attention.
But there she was

                              at second sight,
　　right next to him,
                  her quiet eyes cast down.
　　With stealthy stares
                              I saw her age
　　in her furrowed brow,
                  in the worn wrinkles
　　of her permanent frown.
                  Her lips, I could see,
　　had quavered and cried.
                  (Her tongue, I know,
　　has quarreled—maybe lied.)
                  And I saw her eyes
　　in one minor moment
                      shed their lament,
　　leap from her lap,
                  and lie, instead, on me.
　　And, yes, I saw her
                  features soften then,
　　rapt in some reverie,
                  projecting her lost
　　and latent dreams,
                  correcting all those things
　　that tend to confine
                  with tethering time.
　　But I saw most clearly
                  the space between
　　he   and   she,
                  and with it all of life's
　　brute incongruities
                  mixing and sparring
　　in that cruel chasm of
                              love.

Goodbye

It couldn't have lasted longer than a breath.
No more than a strand of air streaming
down, throughout a knotted throat;
just barely one involuntary intake
in an otherwise inconsequential
lapse in time, in that impossibly
candid intersecting instant—
a final flicker of your face—
Your eyes swollen pink with pain,
pulled down, away from me,
by some strange gravity—
the weight of silent suffering surfacing—
never forgetting what never was.
What a dangerous dependency,
us both regressing to infancy,
trying, failing, not wanting
to wean ourselves off of each other.
Doubly difficult, me seeing that face,
a face that these foolish fingers
never dared to touch. And those
lips—in that one pulse of air,
in that silent transaction,
in that second of sincerity,
yet another missed opportunity,
one last sting of lasting regret,

inhaled, exhaled, in a mournful mouthful—
in just a breath, at a loss for words,
those lips you didn't know I longed for,
cried, contorted in a piteous pout,
parting, like us.

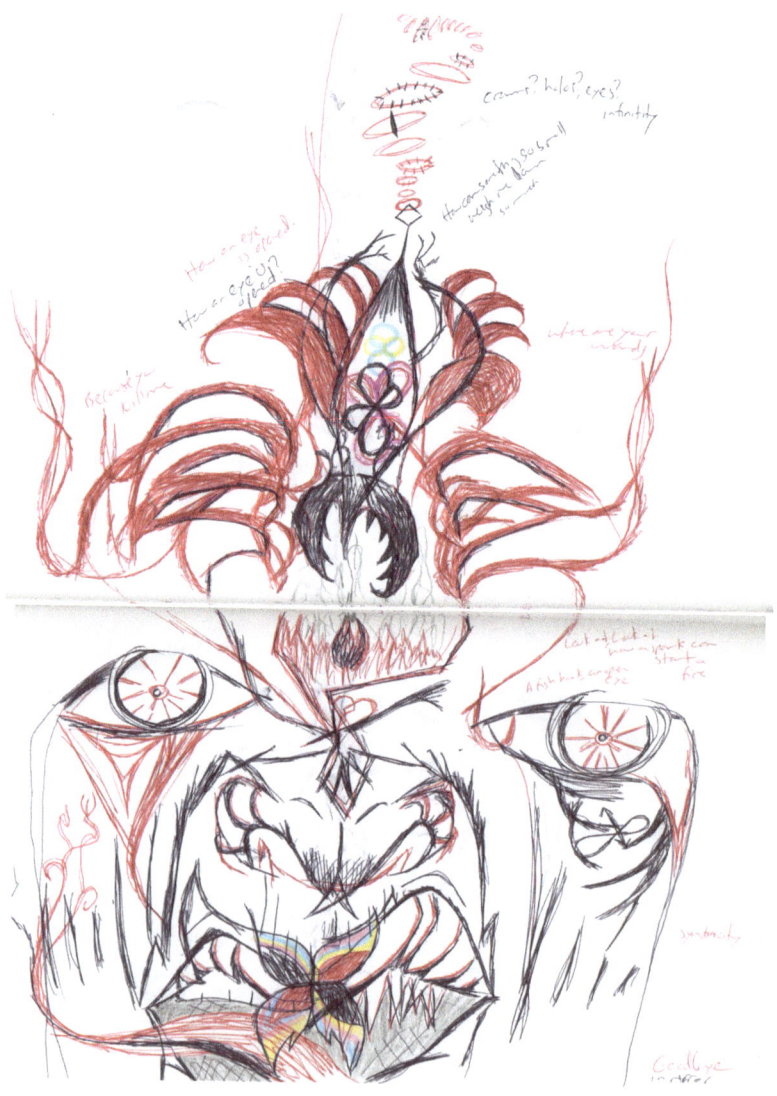

Forgive Me

You knew each
And every
Kind of the
Worst kind of
Loneliness
When you saw
With raw eyes
Every mark,
Every stain,
Every scratch
And blotch on
Your bedroom
Ceiling, all
Feeling lost
In thinking,
Believing
She doesn't
Know or care…
And you're still
Stuck there, still
Thinking I
am clueless,
Unaware
Of your lamp

And it's cold,
　Pale light that
　　Keeps the night
　　　From seeping
　　　　Into your
　　　　　Searing heart.
　　　　　Thinking I
　　　　　Do not know
　　　　　That you keep
　　　　　A picture
　　　　　Of me with
　　　　　You at all
　　　　　Times so you
　　　　Can make the
　　　　　Leaves shudder
　　　　　　With your sighs
　　　　　　Whenever
　　　　　　　You need to.
　　　　　　As if I
　　　　　　Never saw
　　　　　　You avert
　　　　　　Those quiet,
　　　　　Bashful brown
　　　　　Irises
　　　　When I saw
　　　　That sweet blush
　　　　　Of such sweet
　　　　　Attraction
　　　　　Bloom across
　　　　　Your face—soft
　　　crimson fire.
　　As if I

                        Never heard
                    All of that
                    Tremulous
                        Tenderness
                            When your lips
                                Opened and
                                    Gently breathed
                                        Out my name.
                                            As if I
                                                Couldn't feel
                                            It all—all
                                        That harshness,
                                            That sweetness—
                                    In the heat
                                Of your jaw.
                            As if I
                        Didn't know
                    The weight, the
                Pull of that
                One human
            Desire that
        Reduces
    All other
Desires.
Didn't know
That kind of
  Chemistry.
    As if I
        Could even
            Begin to
                Articu-
                    Late what it's

Like when a
Heart palpi-
Tates. As if
Certain things
Aren't always
Mutual.
As If I
Just forgot
Or never
Knew how much
Lush lips can
Crush and kiss
Into 3,
3 measly
Syllables.

Observations of a Generous Man

What is this fascination with your voice?

I remember sitting still and noiseless
As a pond of silver light
And your voice came upon me, stealthily,
Like a breeze or small bird.
And equally as the breeze breathes its own music,
And as a bird births its own song—
A steady current of hum and whisper—
You speak with softness,
Nature's own ventriloquist.
It is immense, yet as unnoticed as
An ant's birth or death—
Your voice's calm sobriety.

And you had no knowledge of this moment
In me, this growth and ascension
Into the sky
When your eyes
(which I am equally fascinated by)
Took me by surprise
                                      And I flew away.

Idle Hands

I watch dusk unravel across the sky as,
I suppose,
every person should at least once
at some point or another,
considering the brevity of a human life.
I move a little, wanting to brush aside the trees
in the distance with the ease that I
sweep away the streaming strand that every so often—
freeing itself from the grip of my ear—
playfully obscures my vision and tickles my nose
as I lay in the grass, raking my slender
fingers through the fine blades,
smoothing one patch in particular,
making it soft and straight,
pretending it's someone else's hair,
(Someone I
Care for very much)
and I remember being younger,
riding in a car with my father
some spring evening,
him looking at the road ahead, his eyes drawn to
the sky while my mind was somewhere else,
as it tends to be, but listening
to him nevertheless, him saying,
"When I look at that, I wish I could paint.

22

If I were more like your mother—"
and I laughed at his old sentiment with my young intuition.
I look and I know
that the difference between then and now
must be the difference between some clumsy words
and a smooth forehead pressed to a car window, soft young
lips forming a warm cloud of breath,
and, I think,
a finger and a finely drawn
smiley face.

Love's True Face

As I Sit Here

he sits there and I think
Amazing—how lives intersect
and complicate each other, fusing
into something like a strange piece of

modern art, some colorful, intricate
mess, like me or him.
The gloom of darkness drifting around the
room matches the bags under his eyes,

those familiar semi-circles something
like those less familiar semi-circles
of kisses. Through the shadows suspended
in loneliness I see that he

has cut his hair. Or did I? I cry
but still can't suppress
a smile
when he smiles.

He stands up too quickly and
doesn't see the stray cord, there,
that trips him up. I watch him
falling

In love? Out of love? Into
something else? Into some space
between people, something as real and
as intimate as the

space between these words, his
eyelashes, or the creases in my
flesh, my mesh of blood and veins?
Fine, dangerous, knotted lines.

Lonely Again

The early sunlight plays along my eyes
(which are still closed, unwilling to embrace
the muffled signs of day that peek and rise
through blinds and creep above me in a maze
of warmth.) And in the pretend darkness of
my mind I can recall your eyes and think
I know the cause of all my troubles…
What can anyone do with a heart that sinks
and leaps so easily? My breath is slow
against my pillow (which feels just like your cheek),
right now only wishing to know
what you're doing, thinking, feeling, weak
with so much wanting, knowing what is practical
has nothing to do with something so fanatical.

An Object of My Affection

There is a clarity in this man's face:
Stillness. In his eyes,
an innocence, an earnestness.
Look at me
like that again.
A cool stream of fire in
the chest—wells up
fills me up cleanly, heavily like sleep
deep deep and exits, slowly,
through my lips as I kiss his
lips quietly to myself. His face
appears, clear and still as snow
unexpected snow
soft as the grayness in the sky
that surrounds distant memories.
No objections, I whisper in my sleep.
No objections to this sweetness, hold close.
Rest your head here awhile, love
echoes restlessly in the
darkness grown white, looking in
through the clear, clear glass.

Communion

Memories move around me like shadows
as I sit in this oppressive room
where nothing moves except the dust
that my breath upsets. My breath,
so soft and hot I see it filling this square
space, a humid presence peeling
off the walls that smell
like mildew and decay. My breath
tastes like the kisses I never got
from him, which is to say, like
nothing. Listen to myself:
nothing. Like silence—I open my mouth
wide to let the silence in and choke
on it like choking in mass on incense or when
white haired Father
Flannigan would tip the cup too
fast. It was full-bodied blood in all
those mouths in Our Lady
of Lourdes parish long before the Pope
perished. No memories are not
shadows. They are fat with blood and color.
Be secret, like love, and rest, I tell
myself, fidgeting with these thoughts.
("Love" is slang to some.
Words of the womb in mothers' mouths,

an inherent part of "lovers."
To others, still, the spilt blood
that stains the floor.) Beauty lives
in stains—and nowhere else.
I watch myself from the
burnt-out fixture in the ceiling
and feel ill, though composed, unlike before—
from now on, inverted like this, a constant
promise to myself. Light, light
my darkness...*Mon Dieu*! How Dark
Times damage! How backwash stings
chapped lips.

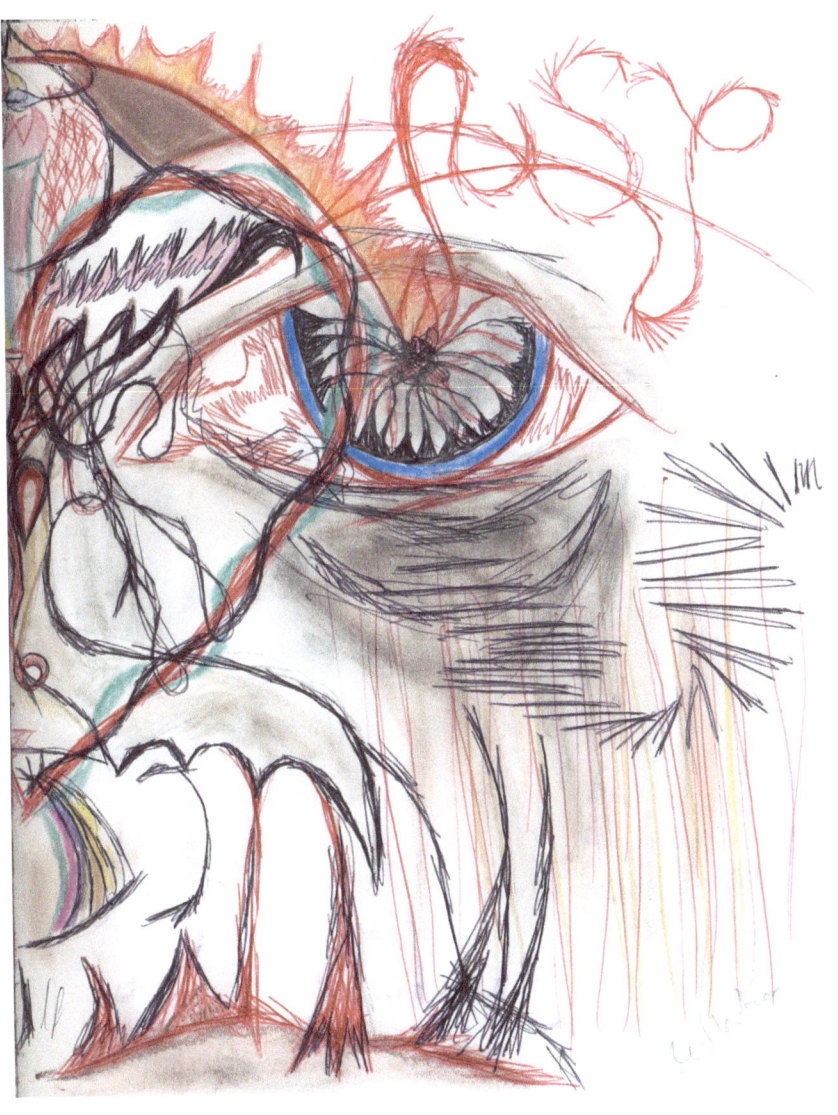

Reflection

Imagine things from these eyes: me
catching my reflection in some glass, catching
all dimensions of my face and the whole
space behind it.

Looking at myself I am foreign
to myself—who is this person that I must
squint to see? Quiet, mouth agape, fast-forward:
watch all dimensions take new form.

What was it that boy saw when he
thought I couldn't feel his eyes all
dewy-sweet on me, a fresh leaf
dwindling?

This face is ripe with two days of tears
over a face it hurts to see, some other leaf
that caught fire and curls into ash and
anger. I pinned his heart—to mine, to me.

While in my own eyes I can't see
myself though I feel my skin exploding
free for once and think
I could love everything.

It is tragic to look out and in
like this and see all the people I could love in life in me
and those I can't
because of unevenly cut circumstance.

Such is My Love

Looking back and through the vague light my memory
gives me, I watch as your love returns, walking towards me,
wading through the dark...(What did you want me to say?)
I can't decipher that love. Too black and thick, that love.
What was that love? The love of eyes? An equilibrium
achieved through gazes, insinuations...A love of eyes,
is that what that was? Knowing how to look at me?
And what about your touch? What about that. I quiver.
Enough about that. So much to say and think (in private)
because of things unsaid in air—the air that is
thick with you. I breathe you in and breathe
you out (such is my love for you), grabbing foolishly,
belatedly for the ghost of my breaths only to watch
them dissolve invisible, intangible, suffocating and precious
like our lovely sadness for each other that was once just--
lovely (once just—love) now rising to the clouds, lost
and drifting towards a softness matched only by our bruises.

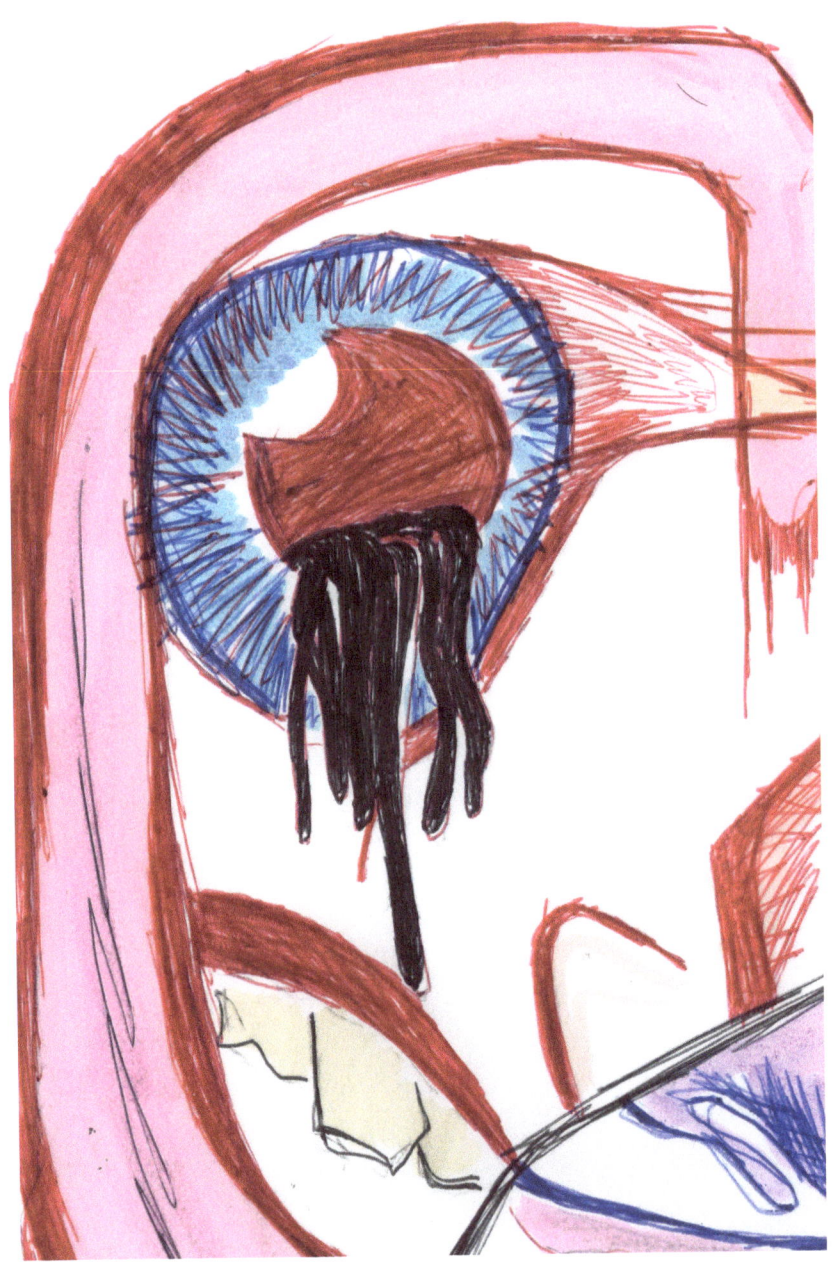

Deprivation

Night
　leaves
　　me alone
　　with
　　myself
　and with a song
　which
　　is equally a
　　　memory and
　　　　that stumbles
　　　　　softly through
　　　　the air, the
　　darkness, my mind
　humid against a
　pillow, awake with
　　alternating feelings
　　　and longings and
　　　　thoughts of
　　　　　bodies
　　　　　　restless in the dark,
　　　　　　wrestling in the dark,
　　　　　wrestling with
　　　　myself, restless
　　　with myself, reckless
　　longing
　for touch (how many
touches
refused, how
　many touches
　　thwarted?
　　　　This touch is all

or nothing.)
   delirious for
    touch, touch
    touch
    touch me *God* like
  Jesus
  healing touch...
Always a collision
on Cartesian planes—
intersecting lines—
parallel, perpendicular,
  the many angles
    of my lust...
      complimentary desires
        desiring each other's
          texture, desiring each
        other's perspiring
      pleasure—
  Reach for me.
  Lonely.
Lovely.
Reach for
Me.
   Slowly
    This music,
  Fingertips
falling on
and in
Me.
  Boldly.

At an Interface

I.

The slow dispersion of the clouds
Across the mind redeem thoughts of you and all
The fear and the explosion of sex and blood
And the fury of dreams…
I linger in the realm of my sin,
The arena of the soul that I am now immured in,
My mind freely floating in those same dissolving clouds,
While my body lingers forever with yours in spring.
    And there was much fear before this love came.
    And there was much violence.
    And then you appeared in my sleep…many times.
Your presence more than a specter and an almost echo of your
    voice
And I could *feel* you.
Yes, you spoke to me, in more than words.

II.

I could *feel* you.
And you felt like the clouds, rising into the sky, one body's
Slow attrition with another.
How can this be? But I love *him*. My heart reminds me in the

>afterthought

Of long and deep thoughts of your incandescent profile (my
>sun).

This poem, this pen, I hope a divination of
Your love, gently encroaching like the night.

III.

And I am torn like the bloody moon as this midnight light
Steals across my face, this page, your bed frame.

Confessions in the Dark

The light from the candles clashes harshly
With your nakedness;
You, something of an infant, a child,
At least in the deep, drumming, thunderous
recesses of your chaste heart,
Which pours its sweet blood like
Wine into my mouth--

I lick your scars, your cuts,
Wounded as we are
By a divine desire forged in fire…
I suck you dry, as if you were fruit.
My body is covered

In thorns, my flowers strewn about the floor
Like garbage or like debris in the aftermath
Of a great storm. Indeed, how superfluous.
The barrier of skin.

--And the perfumes of lust!

The colors of pain saturate the surroundings,
This dungeon of tormented flesh.
There is no room for pretense in this devouring.
Consecrated cannibalism hacking up its entrails,

40

Gruesome and glorious.
The blood pools around my feet.
(When we bleed, we merge.)

And yet, and yet—
Some other part of me objects
And, and—

The light dances on your skin
Like chimes in the wind. Your nakedness
Bewitches, your own concoction of poison.
Where does all this violence
Come from? Your eyes seem to ask.
Passion, of course. But you know how I
Touch, my fingertips like raindrops
Or tears. Pain and love.
These are the only things I understand,
And, I do believe, these fevers of the heart
Are one and the same.

Worn Braille

What was that look you gave me?
That made blush rush to my cheeks?
(A face that knows more of bruises
And scars, love's painful apparitions
Having chiseled heartbreak
Like an epitaph on the tombstone of my face).
What was that stolen glance I wanted
So desperately to return?
What insinuation cloaked your
Features—

And what, what of your reticence?
How also the soft color of your voice,
Its plaintive quiet, its shy eloquence,
Carried by the wind, could not have
Reached my ears in a purer warmth…
(first flush of love…soft touch of light)
What your touch could do…
Given to me stealthily at midnight
When the town sleeps, dreaming in color,
Lovers twisting and clutching, covered in

Rivulets of blankets and moonlight,
Undulations of flesh and light…
(The illumination of a heart's desires!)

Searching each other, t- t- touching…
Bodies slowly softened by familiar
Caresses…make this music last,
Let your lips, wet and warm,
Pink with love's permutations sink,
Like my heart, into song.
Lips so sweet, culling heat,
Fashioning lust and drinking
The tears that have all but
Conquered my countenance.

Watch as they disappear,
A mysterious chemistry.
Enough with the timorousness of looks.
Let our lips stifle speech.
Let them meet and never part
Longer than a whisper's intent.
Let us never be so distant as not
To hear each other's sacred breath,
Reading each other in the blindness
Imposed by the shadows…eyes locked
Or closed, we feel the heat of breath
And body in unison.

Others' hearts are too much tamed
To comprehend such truth.

It Is This Way

What a misbegotten hallucinatory love,
A botch of things, of wreckage and trash,
Of all those things no one wants.
Hallucinatory in that
Not even dreams can fathom it,
For it exists on another plane, like a music.
Misbegotten in that how, how could
This not have happened?
A mishmash of wreckage and trash—
(all those things no one wants or understands)
In that I am that trash, and (and
Let me say that everything grows old even
The stars whose light from these small specks
 Of light seem to never disappear, as midnight
Passes and recalls itself,
Repeats itself, reflects itself. (I have stared
Into the abyss (and seen myself in you
And you in me. In that mirror we are the same,
Complementary, conditional, eternal, sunlight,
Beauty, it all.
(That is the bizarre complexity of it.
You and me. Together. (there is no room
For mixing what is already one))))).—

And that is to say that if I am trash and
We are one, then we both are lost and blowing
In the wind, free and forgotten
Together.

A Seed

Let's begin wherefrom
All beginnings have sprung:
I love you.
Let love spring from love,
Embellished just enough
Bejeweled with the rain that falls
From your eyes when those eyes
Look upon me; look with and within me…
Wherefrom did you come, sweet, sweet sun?
From some explosion within?
Some composition out of combustion?
I can feel your light seep within my skin
Every step closer you get,
(I can feel the steam you emit,
Cauldron of perfumed lust and rain)—
My sun, my cloud, my saint.

A Lullaby
for Sean

Gorgeous dreaming head and eyes and ears
And nose and lips I would like to sing to
Every night with the fading of the light
And all the things that I could give would
Never match all that your life has given the world.
Look outside your little window, hear the little wind blow,
Whistle and chime the faintest of music, and see
The gardens, or where the gardens will be soon.
Watch the flowers grow each day, reach full bloom
In early May; sing to them, like I to you, watch
As they grow, die, renew, and know that I am always
With you. Things grow, things fade, things change,
But I am here like your careful exchange of breath,
Of love, of all true and honest deeds, guiding you,
Helping you, loving you, you'll see.
And when you wake and shine like frost,
Remember love is never lost.

A Lullaby
(Lesson 2)
for Sean

Watch the birds chirping,
Voices bending with the wind
Silent through the glass, whose
Invisible strength is effortless.
Watch and know that they sing for someone
Somewhere, if not for our ears.
Watch and know, watch and learn
That within your heart there burns
Infinite potential, infinite love
And that that love is mirrored above.
Every heart that ever loved
And every breath ever inhaled
And every word ever uttered
Is somehow seen in that
Small song, for instinct is never wrong.
Yes, what is learned can be evil,
What is taught, wrong.
But follow your heart and listen little one,
Lovely little son.

Perennial Forces

Tender apparitional echo
Whereby love grows like a forest,
Or like a stubborn weed—
Dense and unstoppable.
Thickest vegetable love, how I
Hunger for its renewal.
Listen to the wind
(like my heart a million times)
Shudder and the leaves gather in
The gutters like the homeless
Caught in the passageways and in
The sewers…Then love will know
What it means to be the mean.
(And yet, love always knows.)
Steady reverberations sing praise
Of past loves and I am reminded
Of you and how little I can do to stop
The growth of true and innocent
Affection. Honest as a knife
Blade, how does one go about cutting off,
What only grows and grows?
I'm sorry?

Potential Energy

Your heat, your movements are filled
With a soft tenacity
And your heart, a playground for commodious laughter.
    Indeed, when laughter finds its way into your eyes,
        I cry my heart, I cry.
Not for you, although every sweet word formulated on your
even sweeter tongue and every gesture of your hand and it all,
my love, it all is worthy of tears, but for my love
    Which is now burdened by a heavy loss—
        (of a man as beautiful as you…)
Oh, but if I could guide your arms
    To my hips
        And soft skin meeting soft skin
And if we could dance
Or to be married on the moon
Or underwater
Or in the rain, sweet rain
    To be enveloped by *your* heat, to be
        Awakened by *your* touch
            To be…forever.
I could hold you like the air holds me, like the clouds hold the
rain, the sun, light.
        (My sun, my cloud…)
When I saw you I thought *My God, what a beautiful creature!*
    And when you take flight all I can do is marvel at

Your distance from me
    Beautiful ravishing romance
    Of love and loss, of hurt and heat
    Of you and, I hope, of me.

A Christening

His eyes glistened, rimmed with lust, glistened
Like the rain—
      How different from the dew: so thick, so raw,
      Yet equally as new—
The rain glow like the fire glow—those rims of lust—the
      Kindling of the sincerest of affections, abundance—
      Love and lust, and heaven above.
Those leaves, helpless, at the whims of, spurned and fueled
By the wind's innocent flame:
      Beads of sweat and light mix and become
indistinguishable—
      Two blue beads, mirrors or your sentiments,
privations, fantasies:
      Your dreams.

52
The purity of heat and rain—fertility, fecundity
>	Love as thick and rich as soil
>	Four points diamond-like shining quick like
>	Lightening in the expanse of the black fragile night
>	Stealing the wreckage away of a battered tattered
tortured
>	Crying thing that lives within a
>	Ring of heat—of heat and lust and rain.
>	>	And the wind's flame seduces the demons
inside of
>	>	Me, and I move with them.
>	Teach me how—
>	>	Teach me how to forget—
>	>	>	To forget it all again.

A Transient Anger

It is dead

    Said some trickle of infinitesimal thought deep inside
    The debris of my destitute head.

I have thought of him and thought of him
The way he smiles like a curve of moon
The way he laughs like a folk tune or like daylight
    Jabbing
        at the darks of afternoon

And I have only thought and I was never meant to think
But to feel and to be in motion with and to collide with and to
    betray such feelings as if
      By a divine force, or by instinct.
I've had enough of these soothsaying dreams, his voodoo
    (In dreams he makes his daring moves
    Pummeling through
        Stretching me like rubber glue
    To feel the mutual tumult of our electricity.)

No I was not meant to think of anything but the religion of
    Keats

    And the spinning stars that have proved
       Better company than him
Only coming out at night, too
          But at least they're closer,
          Yes, much closer to this lost moon

Catch 22

Or maybe yes—
> I think there is a possibility that I might love you.
>
> That I might be in love with you.

(How can this be? Feelings so deep they must have been concealed from me—)

Sure, I say one thing, but I mean another.

Truly, my blood sings for you.

(Between us the smoothest friction I will ever feel.)

This is not work, not for me—

For me, this is play.

> *(Even though you are a prisoner here,*
>
> *In my heart, where flowers bloom like bruises*
>
> *And the scars of an inner violence proliferate?)*

You try to save me, and you do, *without* trying—

> Just by looking at me and giving me your
>
> Handsome face, for a second.

(Indeed, this seems a cruel yet artful striptease…)

Where I strip and you tease?

Of course I play games. Of course I entertain desire with imagination—

For each word is a consummation of imagination and desire, immaculate in origin—

And listen:

Pride of my one true heart,

    You speak in rich colors,

    Rich and dark

        and that music

    Moves me; my mind dances

    In tune with *your* dizzying moves

    Your eyes that soothe

    And all other attributes:

    Hair skin and daring mysterious

    Magnetism.

Ah, heal me, work your magic, and never see me again.

(If I see you again, you will be my prisoner—)

Neither fate is fortunate.

But if you believe in me, you will see me at your doorstep,

Free as the clouds, as the stars, as all things untouched by man,

    Begging, begging for a

        Kiss.

Death By A Thousand Cuts

Wearing scars like jewelry, fresh, raw, ruby red
(and with the price of blood) the body knows itself—
Its weaknesses, its power, felt with the depth of each
    incision…

The body. That canvass of pain. What meaning can be
    resurrected
From rotten, labyrinthine intestines and the festering heat of a
sun that scorches cheeks, the coarse cracks and

furrows of mud and faces, mixing—faces scored with scars
    like skated ice
Or like most things that breathe and die—faces eroding
and withering into their own disfigurement, as age and
    decrepitude

Dismantle our bones. Displaced fear lurks like a stalker
In the shadows that we have created: The bald walls of prison
    cells house
Uniquely human vices, while outside we are led blindly to
    believe

In our false purity…The soul lives at a razor's edge
Rusted and worn with time and suffering. Pain: we are closer

to God by it.
People become vermin, the prey of power, spitting sin

like venom, poisoning their own. Death loiters in the cobwebbed
Corners of rooms we dare not enter. Hot blood curdles in intemperate veins,
Where blood longs to reunite with blood, back to the womb, back to the womb

Free from all these wounds. Footsteps echo in haunted hallways
Where dead stories rekindle their power. The living world is filled with ghosts.
Naked bodies learn living death sacrificed by filthy hands,

Crawling like maggots and lice…We pray for forgiveness…
A chunk of skin, seething blood, stained and mottled flesh mesh
With heat and softened earth, entering all the natural world's

Processes…dead voices rasp in the night.
Pleas sting God's gut. The wind thrashes through the leaves,
where love is forgotten and dies. The sickness descends from the

Bleeding sky. We are not immune to sin. Branches twist and writhe
Like worms, thunderous clouds swarming like wasps.
The sky, a poignant purple, bruised by man and by God's demands.

Mouths open to scream, inhaling, exhaling poisoned plumes, feeling the delicate
Spirals of pain…Will we ever know freedom?
Sores swell and bodies bloat. Great roots reach scraps of clothes,

Clumps of hair where the earth has been torn. The line that separates life from
Death as great as the divide between two opposing eternities,
while as tenuous as a breath, as delicate as a barely audible pulse

Of blood. The legion of creatures that stir in the earth and mingle with
Dead things deny us eternity, their dirt as cold as the corpses.
 It is all lost to madness.
Words flame up when lit by a pair of eccentric eyes…

Words we return to. Words that connect us like the sinews and tendons
Of the nightmarish bodies we are trapped in. God broods in the clouds.
His ancient, cold and broken stares slash like knives.

Finally, our eyes dim. Our pain is each other's pain.

A Diminished Thing

I'm tired.
My brain is mute and sick
And retches.

And I have stared at this
Indifferent, colorless abyss
For far too long.

And I just *can't* force what isn't there.
And I have nothing to give this time
Except

A few little blotches
Of sorry imperfection,
A trickle of my frustration,

Some salty, stinging, redundant
Truth falls, bleeds
Through in a pathetic

Flood: That futile, frantic fray
Of pen against
Paper—

Because sometimes paper
Is a rough substitute
For tissue

And because I have yet to learn
How to talk like
Tears.

www.ingramcontent.com/pod-product-compliance
Lightning Source LLC
Chambersburg PA
CBHW042044290426
44109CB00001B/29